THE DAY WE
BECAME ME

THE DAY WE BECAME ME

Dr. Sal J. Pellicano

Xulon Elite

Xulon Press Elite
2301 Lucien Way #415
Maitland, FL 32751
407.339.4217
www.xulonpress.com

Unless otherwise indicated, Scripture quotations taken from the American Standard Version (ASV)-public domain

Printed in the United States of America.

Edited by Xulon Press

ISBN-13: 9781545625873

This book is in memory of Bette Lou Pellicano, or as I knew her, Grandmom.

I still remember the day you lost your battle to cancer. I walked in my mom's room only to hear her heart-wrenching cries. I was so young at the time and could have never imaged the way your passing would still affect me today; one week after my 22nd birthday. But I try not to think about that horrific day. Instead, I think about all the beautiful memories we shared.

I think about the many times I woke up to find you sitting outside, reading the bible. I remember all the stories you read to me, and all that I learned. Because of those memories and lessons, I credit you with my salvation. I remember the many times you showed love and care to animals. I recall watching you in awe and disbelief as you showed a wounded turtle we found on the side of the road the same kind of love you showed me. I accredit my adoration for animals to you, and so does everyone else.

I remember your consistent happiness and admiration for life itself. Looking back, I truly cannot believe how strong you were. You knew you didn't have much longer in this life, but I do not have any memories of you in sorrow or sadness. I used to wonder why God took you from me at such a young age. Why I had to grow up most of my life without a Grandmom, but now I think I understand. Your teachings and influences would take most people two lifetimes to accomplish, but you did not need that kind of time. Even though most of my years have been spent without you, you are never far from me. Your wisdom and grace will stay with me forever. I am not sad you were taken from us so young, but blessed that we had the time we did. I am who I am, because of you. Your memory will forever live on. I love you, Grandmom. I will see you soon.

-Kaitlyn

TABLE OF CONTENTS

FUNNY THING ABOUT getting old, you don't
look any older, until you stand in front of a mirror, and
you feel good, until you try to stand. There is at least
one advantage of growing older—the experiences that
are accumulated during the process. My assessment
of life is that experiences, good, or bad, if permitted,
may define that life. Please consider, there is so much
more to an individual than the experiences he or she
has enjoyed, or perhaps suffered. I will, however, con-
cede experiences do hold a significant place in our lives.
This account is proof of that last statement.

Like everyone, I have "experiences," some wonderful, some not so wonderful: the death of my wife
in 2004 was the most difficult. The news that my oldest
son would never walk again, follows in severity. Sure,
I've had my share of sorrow. I have also enjoyed many
happy experiences: the birth of each of my six children,

the relationship I have with Jesus Christ, the level of health I enjoy, and of course my current marriage with Karen. Happiness is more than an emotion or sensation: it is a decision, a choice. I grew up watching my mother choose misery, in an otherwise good life; consequently, she spent much of her life in mental institutions. But that's the subject of another book.

There have been several bad experiences I have suffered, but one effected a terror that is beyond my ability to describe. It's true my wife's death caused tremendous trauma, but it was expected, and there was a measure of the conventional—we all must die. This experience revealed an evil that was more than the limits my mind could grasp; this event was spiritual, and I was made aware of how insignificant and defenseless I was in confronting it. It changed my life like nothing else. To this day, my skin crawls when I bring it back to my memory.

How well I remember pleading, "Please God help me." It's about two a.m. and I am terrified. I have never been so panicked in my life, I'm trembling uncontrollably. They're here, I know they are, but I can't see them. "Oh God help me." It's been thirty years, but that night will forever remain with me. Sure, some of the details have become faint, or blurred, but what happened to me in that bedroom, I wish I could forget.

This story begins much earlier, some fifteen years earlier. It's 1970, and I'm living in New Jersey. I have a successful custom motorcycle business. I have a wonderful wife and, at that time, I had four great kids. Unfortunately, the nature of my business caused me some troubles, but I was young, I thought I was tough, and I was more than willing to mix it up if it came to that. Things were going great. I enjoyed all the amenities, great family, nice house, and things were great financially. What a life!

For five years, I convinced myself that I was smarter than most, and tougher than most. I reasoned; who else my age had what I had, and I earned it. I did it! It was me that bought that new Lincoln, and it was me who bought the new car my wife was driving. Every year we spent a month in Florida; I made that possible. I was at the top of my game. I arrived. I was there!

I was so full of me, there was very little room for anyone else. I went where I wanted to go, did what I wanted do, bought what I wanted to buy and be damned if anyone didn't like it. It wasn't, however, as good for my wife. For years, she endured my arrogance and deceit. Every night she knelt next to the side of the bed praying for her narcissist husband. The first few years, her prayers and her endurance angered me; I wasn't going to change, why should I? Seeing her there, with her head resting on her arm, praying; it was, well, demoralizing. Months turned into years; her persistence grew to be annoying. Every night the same thing; she prayed, and I lay there. Before long her incessant prayers became uncomfortable. If I happened to walk past our children's bedroom at bedtime, I would hear, "Don't forget to pray for daddy".

Inside of me, something was happening. I was changing: new cars no longer made me as happy as they once did; I bought three new Lincolns in less than 18 months, each one more expensive than the one before. Even the motorcycle I had custom built did nothing for me. It was a beauty; *Touring Bike* magazine used it as it's centerfold. It seemed that nothing could make me happy. I was miserable. I wanted so badly to be happy, to have the joy that I once had.

THAT NIGHT

---•---

As Bette slipped under the sheets, her eyes were fixed on mine, and this time I didn't turn away. In the past I was careful not to allow our eyes to meet. I feared they would betray who I was, and what I had become, but now I was to the point of desperation; my need overcame my fear. The bad, tough guy attitude was gone, replaced with an overwhelming emptiness. My arrogance was replaced with overwhelming need. I was in tears. "When will you come back?" Bette asked.

When will I come back? With all I had: my fancy cars, fast motorcycles, tough guy attitude, money, yet inside I was broken. Would He take me back? Was there anything salvageable? It wasn't so long ago that I had recognized my need for God, and I asked Him to save me from my sin. But my success together with my desire for the world caused me to walked away from God; I

1

chose sin. I walked away from God. I had no need for God. I had gone so far that I began to doubt the existence of God. I reasoned, my business success was due to my exceptional abilities. Stuff was what I wanted, and stuff was what I got. Next was freedom. No restrictions are what I demanded, and for a while I thought I attained that freedom. I believed I was there, but I wasn't. The freedom I pursued only worked to enslave me. Emptiness and poverty of spirit overwhelmed me. (WCF Chapter 18.4)

Bette knew! When our eyes met, she knew, but how much did my eyes reveal? I will never know, and now added to my unbearable need, included shame, and humiliation. Before too much was revealed, I closed my eyes, hopeful to conceal my infamy, but when I reopened them, I was not met with anger, not even resentment. No, Bette's eyes expressed compassion. Unconditional love is what I saw. How could she love me? Why would she love me? Her face was now wet with tears; as wet as mine. She rose, and walked to my side of the bed, she softly touched my arm, and we knelt together. With her arm around me, I begged for her forgiveness, and mercifully she did. I then I begged for the forgiveness of my Father, and I knew without doubt He, too, forgave me. The prodigal had come home. That night I felt His arms around me, and as I had done so many times with my children, I could sense Him say, "It's okay, it's okay, it will be alright." To express in words all that I felt that night would be impossible, but I knew it was alright. I was forgiven.

Reconstruction

———————◆———————

MONTHS EARLIER A trip to Daytona, FL. had been planned. A week had been set aside to enjoy the annual motorcycle races. Joe, Paul and James boarded my motorhome and we were off to the races. My heart wasn't into going; I was still basking in my Father's forgiveness, and I wanted to be home with Bette and my kids, but the plans had been made many months ago. They knew something was different: I was quieter, more reserved, when they made off color remarks, I would say nothing or look in a different direction. They were baffled, maybe even a little concerned.

About fifty miles from Daytona, the sky darkened, and the rains came. It rained so much, and so long the race had to be called. Heading back to New Jersey was not an option. A week in Florida was planned, and they wanted some "fun in the sun." They were aware I knew my way around Florida. "Hey man," they whined, "we got plenty of time, let's go someplace and have some fun." My definition of fun had changed, but I was very familiar with theirs. Off to Key West. I reasoned the trip to Key West would take at least two days, maybe three. Time spent driving was a plus. The count-down to getting back home was crucial, and long periods of driving meant less time with the possibility of getting into trouble.

It was evening when we rolled into Key West. Duval Street, and people were everywhere. Duval Street is always bustling unless there's a threat of a hurricane. The guys spotted a bar they thought needed their patronage. The parking lot was big enough to accommodate all 32 feet of my motorhome, and that's where we spent the next five hours. Any doubt that I had changed was eliminated when I told them that I would wait for them in the motorhome. "Come on man, it's a topless bar," Paul demanded. I stood my ground; they went in shaking their heads and grumbling.

While they were in the bar, I decided It would be a good time to read. Try as I may, I just couldn't concentrate. I know I read the same chapter in the Bible four times, and had no idea what I had just read. Frustrated, I quit trying, and decided I needed to talk with God. More accurately, He wanted to talk to me. That night was very significant; it was about my future; it was a full docket. "Dear Heavenly Father," I began, but somehow I knew "Heavenly Father" wasn't hearing me, or didn't want to listen to me. Don't ask how I knew, but I had no doubt. Then the questions began: is He angry with me because I'm here instead of with my family. Maybe it's because I'm sitting in the parking lot of a topless bar. I followed that line of reasoning for a while. "Lord," I asked, "are you angry with me?" I was relieved; no thunder, and no lightening. I have told this story only twice, and on both occasions, it sounded a little bizarre. Now that I am putting it down on paper, it sounds ridiculous, but I promise, it is the truth, so help me God!

Well, I concluded God was not angry with me, I was relatively confident of that conclusion, but the question remains: how do I acquire the attention of

God? Wow! What a question? The answer was instantaneous. No pause and no delay.

To this day, I wish I could explain the events of that evening. My dialog with the Sovereign God was confusing to me even as it was occurring. I remember thinking; "this isn't happening," but I could not deny that it most certainly was! I am incapable of a rational explanation of that night, and I would learn that rational doesn't always find a place in the realm of the spiritual. I have learned that there are a lot of things that have happened in my life that I have no understanding. For some of those "things" I am grateful.

The words, "I want you" kept recurring in my mind. I was having some difficulty with the question. Was God talking to me in that small still voice that I had read about in first Kings 19:12?

>"And after the earthquake a fire; but the
> LORD was not in the fire:

>and after the fire a still small voice.

My answer was somewhat tentative, "But Lord you have me." Again, the voice, this time it was more of a directive; "I want **you**." I was beginning to understand what was happening. It was the "stuff." All the "stuff," I reasoned, was an impediment or obstacle; I did love my "stuff." I was slowly getting the hang of this. It took a little while, but I was okay with giving the Lord my toys. I answered with as much humility as I could muster, "Lord, if that's it, if it is all of those things that I have accumulated, I gladly offer them to you: my cars, and my motorcycles, my tools, and yes Lord my motorhome." Confident that everything was good now, I relaxed. Yet again that voice, "I want you!" Without doubt, this was getting serious, very serious, and I was beginning to get very uncomfortable. No! I can give more than what I have already given. I knew where God was taking me, and I wasn't wanting to go there. "I have given You everything," I argued. He has me, and all my "stuff." Okay, okay, "Father, I said," as pious a voice as I could muster, "my business is yours." Before I ever mouthed those words, I knew that wasn't enough, there's more, much more. Again, I reasoned, this is foolishness. This is a fantasy, it's not happening. "I want you!" No, no, no, please don't ask for my children. What if He decided to take my children? Oh, no, I can't even begin to think about that. No, I can't, please don't ask that. Pacing, back and forth in the confines of that small area, I kept thinking how awful it would be. These are my children; I can't do it. Surely, that's too much to ask of a man. Through all the reasoning, and all the tears, and all the pacing, I knew where this was going to end, and I also knew I was powerless to stop it. I relented, "Okay, my children are yours to do with as you wish." Who was I kidding. Certainly, not God. For over an hour I reasoned and bargained, and even begged. "I want you!" Again, those words, those same damned words, but this time they came as no surprise, and there was no need to expand on them. I knew it was coming.

There was nothing more important to me than my wife. She was my world, my present, and my future. It was she that kept me from self-destruction. She was my life! I knew how important she was to me, and so did God. No amount of reasoning would persuade God otherwise. To me, Bette was non-negotiable, but to God, she was the finale. From the first "I want you" to the last it was Bette He wanted me to offer.

I just sat there considering the consequences, and the effects of my life without my precious wife. Certainly, I knew He could take her anytime He decided, but would God do such a thing? He knew I wasn't strong enough. I would never be strong enough, never! It had been hours since this ordeal began, and I was exhausted. I had been wrestled with the Almighty, and like many before me, He was the victor. Can a mere man overcome God? O, foolish man that I am. Finally, and agonizingly I gave my answer, the only answer I could give, "Father, she is yours to take if that is your will, but I beg; please permit her to remain with me," that was it. The objective completed. I knew for some time that it was Bette this whole exercise was about.

Following my salvation experience, I had, without realizing, erected barriers affecting my relationship with the Almighty: being successful, having things— cars, motorcycles, popularity, etc. I firmly believed I was where I wanted to be, but the greatest impediment, strangely enough, was my extraordinary love for Bette. Ridiculous as that may sound, I believe it to be a valid evaluation. The pedestal I had positioned for my wife was much higher than my reverence, and love for God. It is my belief Adam suffered that same offense. He allowed his love for Eve to eclipse his love for God. The Bible tells us that Eve was deceived in the garden, but Adam was not in 2 Cor. 11:3, indicating he ate of the fruit willingly and knowing his action was a deliberate act of defiance against God; Adam's desire for Eve was greater than his love and loyalty for his creator. Anything, or anyone an individual elevates above God, compromises the faith of the individual, and he or she will fall. Luke 14: 26-28 informs us where our loyalty and love must be.

> "If any man come to me, and hate not his father, and mother, and wife, and children, and brethren, and sisters, yea and hisown life also, he cannot be my disciple."

As the evening was concluding, I came to understand that God wanted me to expand my education, that would include Biblical training. God wanted me to go back to school, why, I could only guess, but I agreed. Whatever it was that God wanted of me I vowed I would do. I did make one request. "Lord if it be Your will, please allow me to move to Florida." That was it! I gave God my word. I would do as He asked. Oh, what a night!

An interesting sidebar: the guys staggered on board, and we started on our way. We were on our way in search of a campground to spend the night. We had travelled four or five miles on Highway 1 when a State policeman pulled me over. The officers first question was, how much have you had to drink? "Officer, I don't drink so I've had nothing to drink." "Sir," he began, "I have been parked across the road, and I have observed this motorhome parked at that bar for at least two hours. I also saw you and two other men get into this motorhome. Would you want to change your story?" When I smiled, I couldn't help notice his ire elevate. "Officer," I began, "you did see three men enter this motorhome, but I was not one of them. If you like I will have my friends come out." The officer realized I was being truthful, and stated that would not be necessary. He went on to explain that he could not allow a vehicle the size of mine to cross the seven-mile-bridge believing it was being driven by someone who was under the influence. I thanked him for his diligence, and we went our separate ways. The seven-mile-bridge, at that time, was extremely narrow. It was common for big trucks to hit and break their mirrors as they crossed from opposing directions.

All, who acknowledge the Almighty know there is a plan for their lives, and I was certainly not immune from that blueprint, but what place would I provide. Instantaneously, a memory: It was 1963, I was eighteen years old. As I drove across the railroad tracks, I heard a voice. It was the first time I heard that voice. It said that I was to be a minister. There was no one in the back seat; therefore, I must be crazy, but it happened again. That was an impossibility! I had lost all faith in God, and was convinced such a being did not exist. Therefore, the possibility of me being a minister of God was absolute foolishness. God, I argued, was for the weak. Nevertheless, I heard it! That experience was so significant that to this day I remember the exact month, it was February. I remember the exact place, it was on highway 47 in Glassboro, NJ. The year was 1963, and the car was my 1962 Chevy, Impala. I even remember it was early evening.

After a good laugh, I tried to dismiss what happened, but never did. The only one I had ever told about that evening was Bette, and I didn't tell her about it until that night, the night I came back. Could it be that God was calling me to the ministry? I was a lot of things minister wasn't one of them.

OLD HABITS

———————•———————

IT WAS A great spring. Business was good and growing, and as for me, I was a happy man! There were still a few customers who were a problem. A small number of my clientele included some who were members of gangs: The Warlocks, the Wheels of Soul, and the Pagans. There was one major difference between me and them. I thought I was tough; they were indisputably tough. To gain some advantage, I believed a gun would even the score. Who was I kidding; they all carried guns. Point of fact, a photo of the Wheels of Soul was displayed in the Woodbury Times, a local newspaper. In that photograph, all the members of the gang were brandishing a gun.

A good friend, Danny V., came for a visit. Danny was a big man; 6' 3," and about 200 pounds of solid muscle. He worked as a bouncer in a club in Camden, NJ. He looked at my new 357 Magnum and politely asked, "Do you know what this gun can do to a man? Do you honestly think you can point this thing at a man trying to rob you and pull the trigger?" Ready to give my answer, he stopped me and demanded, "Think about it before you answer." Finally, I gave my answer, no, I could not! Not unless I were certain my life or the lives of my family were in jeopardy; no, I couldn't. Until, this writing, the following events have never been revealed. It was my first-time deer hunting. There were three of us; Joe, Harry, and me. We were about fifty yards apart. Sitting there, shivering, and admiring my new 12-gauge shotgun, I looked to my right and there not thirty feet from me was a beautiful deer. He was looking away providing me with a great shot. I trained my gun on the him, but I just couldn't pull that damn trigger. He was such a handsome animal. I just couldn't kill him. To make certain Joe or Harry didn't get a shot, I raised my brand-new Remington 12-gauge pump action shotgun upward and I fired. I was learning about "Me."

As the season slowed, it gave me time to reflect on that night in the motorhome. Did God want me to become His minister? All the ministers I knew were, well, they weren't "manly;" they were kind of, how can I say it—weak, girlish, sweet, not tough! They were nice! I wasn't! In fact, an argument could be made that I was a little abrasive. "Well, that's it!" I concluded, "I'm not going to be a minister; besides, I'm too much of a...butt."

So, what am I going to do about my parley with God. After much consideration, I decided that selling out would afford me enough money to move to Florida. My business was doing quite well and had to have considerable value. Then there were my many toys, three or four motorcycles, just my customized Gold Wing had to be worth a bundle. Much of it was done in 24k gold, the wheels were specially ordered and I had them plated in black chrome, not to mention everything else that had been done to it. Over the years I had accumulated numerous tools, and, of course, there was my inventory of parts and accessories. Yes, sir I was worth a bundle, and since houses in Florida were much less expensive than in NJ., I could buy a nice place, relax a little, and then I would look around for a Bible college to attend. I now had a plan.

Well, giving up so much was more difficult than I realized. Florida was a great place to vacation, but to move there? I was having second thoughts. Why can't I serve God right where I am? That way I can keep my business, my money, and my all important "stuff." Plan B.

On one of our trips to Florida, I bought a small house. It was an older home in need of a lot of repair, but it was cheap. When I bought it, my thinking was to have it insulated and central air conditioning installed. Over time, I would have it completely remodeled. There was always the possibility of using it as a rental. I was so proud of myself, there was just no limit to my genius!

The church, Bette and I attended, in New Jersey, was small and friendly. Pastor H was a great guy, and we got along well. His faith in me increased, so much that he asked me to teach a Sunday school class. A short time passed, and I was asked to serve as a deacon. Spiritually, I was doing well. Winters were traditionally a slow time for the motorcycle business in NJ; it was too cold to ride. That gave me a great opportunity to study the Bible. Soon bookcases had to be built to house the volumes of books on theology I was acquiring. There was so much to learn; I had no idea how much. Ever so slowly, I was learning that I wasn't as brilliant as I once believed. It was through learning I realized how rash and imprudent I was. Spiritually, I was doing well, my business, however, was not. Competition was increasing; Even K-Mart began selling motorcycle parts. It seemed there were motorcycle shops opening all around me. My trusted mechanic, I learned, was using drugs; consequently, the work he produced was inferior. If I were to turn things around, it had to be done quickly. It became clear, it was time to sell some stuff. My motorhome was the first fatality, next my motorcycles. Things were not so good; it was a troubling time for me. The "dialogue" I had with God in the motorhome had long been forgotten. Believing my relationship with God was good, I had moved on, but I was in trouble financially, and I was running out of options.

21

To add to my situation, I was having problems with the new pastor the church installed. He was a very young man who rejected advise. Of course, I was the young man who demanded he listen to the advice of the deacons, of which I was one. It seems one of the Sunday-School teachers was seeking a divorce from her physically abusive husband. (Bruises were often visible, including black-eyes.)

At the monthly deacons meeting, it was decided— with one exception--the Sunday-School teacher should be asked to resign. The reasoning: since she taught children it would set a bad example. The decision was about to be rendered, when I asked if I might be allowed to offer my remedy. "As you know," I began, "I own a motorcycle business, as such, I on occasion, meet some very unsavory individuals." "Recently," I continued, "one of my customers suggested, if I had anyone who needed to be 'taken care of' I could count on him to see to it." "What does that have to do with anything here?" Dave asked, somewhat annoyed. "Let me finish," I demanded. "I could call this customer, and ask that he 'take care of' our Sunday-School teacher's husband, and if she found herself short on funds to make it happen, we could use the deacons fund to cover it." The look on the deacons' faces was priceless. They were certain I had lost my mind. But, I wasn't done. I went on to give the punch-line. "After all," I reasoned, "we can offer forgiveness for murder, but we could not offer forgiveness for divorce." Unfortunately, there was no discussion on the substance of my remarks. In fact, I wondered if they thought I was serious. Our Sunday-School teacher was asked to resign. She did, and she also resigned from the church. There were many other instances I thought were injurious to the church. Bette and I decided to resign. Unfortunately, the church went downhill quickly, and closed its doors not long after.

Bette and I talked, and we prayed. We talked until we were worn out from talking. We decided to move to that small house I had purchased in Florida. No improvements had been made since I had purchased it; I just never got around to it. Bette was excited; I was worried. Was I doing the right thing? Two of our six children had married, but the remaining four would be moving with us to Florida. Bette's parents

THE DAY WE BECAME ME

lived not far, but they were the only people we knew. How was I going to support my family? Even through all the turmoil, I realized this was the right move. No! there were no voices this time, but I knew this was what God wanted. All my wonderful toys were gone. Worse, much worse, I was financially ruined, and I had no job! I was panic stricken, Bette was, well, content. She knew, without doubt, everything was going to be fine; maybe she was hearing "small voices." If she was, she never told me. Having observed my mother those many times, I recognized that I was entering a state of depression. Repeatedly, I demanded of myself, "Stop, pull yourself together." Once again, the prayers of my Bette got me through.

We found a great little church, and once again the pastor, James D, and I got along very well. Jim knew we were having a hard time; we were barely making it. One afternoon Jim drove into the driveway; he greeted me with his usual exuberance. "Hey, Sal, how are you? Can you give me a hand here?" "Sure," I answered. There in his van were four boxes of food. Smiling broadly, Jim explained, "The groceries come from the deacon's fund for folks who need a little help. My mind was screaming, "NO! NO! NO!" Has it come to this, I thought? Am I now reduced to accepting CHARITY? NO! I couldn't look at Jim. I was so ashamed, so humiliated. How could this have happened? I was always the one who gave to those in need. Now, it's me? NEVER! "Jim," I managed to say, "I can't accept this." "Sal," he began, "Would these groceries help you?" "I guess so," was my answer." "Then why are you refusing them? Is it pride, is that what it is? Will you deny the church a blessing from God, or worse will you deny God whose instruction I believe, we are following?" Learning humility is hell! I thanked pastor Jim, and apologized for my elevated vanity. Both Bette and I found work, that, too, was humiliating for me. Bette had been a stay-at-home-mom for almost all our married years.

It was customary for pastor Jim to end his messages with an invitation to salvation, and this Sunday morning he remained consistent. In addition to the call to salvation was an additional bidding, one that I had never heard Jim extend before. "If there is anyone here this morning," Jim started, "who has made a promise or vow to God, and yet has not fulfilled that promise? Please come to the front of the sanctuary. I would like to have a word with you." "No!" I said inaudibly, "He didn't just say that, did he?" How could Jim know about the vow I made so many years ago? He never extended an invitation like that before, did he? With a very red face, I walked to the front of the sanctuary. Knowing our conversation would likely be a long one, Jim asked to meet with me some evening to talk.

Satisfied with my answers, Jim informed me of a college he knew and thought highly of. He also offered to take me there to share my story with the dean. I reminded Jim of my financial condition, to which he just smiled and added," God would find a way," but I didn't hold much hope. I had no money, none, and I was in debt. It took every penny of our combined salaries just to survive: food, utilities, mortgage, a van payment, the needs of our four children; there was nothing left. How could I consider going away to college, a college that was hours away? There was housing, and books, and countless other expenses. It was impossible! It was ridiculous, and I needed to stop thinking about it.

The sooner I would learn to accept my "station" in life the better. Besides, I was never a good student. Bette didn't have much to say about my going to school or our current situation. She didn't have a lot to about anything; she was a naturally quiet person. Bette never complained, or argued. She certainly would have been justified, but never did. Bette had an unshakable faith, a faith that acknowledged the absolute control of a Sovereign God. Bette was content with her place with God, *"Not that I speak from want, for I have learned to be content in whatever circumstances I am" (Philp. 4:11).* I hadn't learned that yet; I don't know that I ever will.

FROM BIKER TO BAKER

BETTE AND I both had found work at the new marketplace that opened near where we lived. We worked in the bakery department. While Bette did well, I hated it. Bette just rolled with the punches; I blocked and wanted to punch back. Working for someone was relatively new for me. When I was treated unfairly, I didn't like it, but I took it. I had no choice, I was desperate for the job. Did I mention "learning humility is hell?" Shaking that tough guy, New Jersey, Sicilian attitude was going to be very difficult. It still is!

Most of the employees were females, and I did enjoy working with the ladies. They would tease Bette and I about our up-north accent, and we would tease back about their southern customs and vernacular. The question might be asked; how, did I go from biker to baker? It's the other way around. My father and his father were both bakers. Grandpop learned to bake from an uncle in Sicily. In the early 1900's the family migrated to the US. My father looked to be about four or five, judging from the photos I saw. Grandpop opened a bakery in Philadelphia, PA, and that's where my dad learned to bake. Following natural progression, my dad opened a bakery in New Jersey and that's where I learned to bake. Baking was my vocation all through high school and continued for the first couple of years of our marriage. Wow! I did it, one hundred years of history in a paragraph.

Because of my background in baking, I was being groomed to be manager. The current manager was hired out of desperation—the company was enjoying a growth spurt and had no one else to manage the new bakery. Bill, the current manager, could barely read; consequently, he depended on me for everything—ordering supplies, making work schedules, hiring new employees, even making out the daily production list. Bill, may have been ignorant, but he wasn't stupid, he knew after I fulfilled my one year probation, he would be transferred or demoted, and I would become the manager; consequently, even though he desperately needed me, his dislike for me was intense, and that made my life hell. Everyone in the bakery department knew how much Bill depended on me. They also knew how much he detested me. Any questions asked of Bill, he would seek me out for the answers. Eventually, the employees recognized that it was me who was answering their questions; consequently, Bill was bypassed, and the question would come directly to me. Bill became aware of what was happening, and ruled that no one was to speak to me. It was awful, but it was all in the plan of God. Oh, how I hated to go to work. On many an occasion, I thought I would vomit on the way. Did I mention anything about humility?

One of our hires was a girl named Sherry. She adapted well, and was quick to learn. I was amazed how quickly she learned how use the machinery. Sherry and I worked well together. Apparently, Sherry told her parents about the couple from New Jersey, and we were invited to their home to visit. They were great folks, but they were both troubled about their rebellious daughter. Over the months we became quite friendly.

Sherry's mother called one evening, as she had done on many occasions. During our conversation, she asked if I would pray for her daughter, and maybe, if I would, keep an eye on her she would appreciate it. She was worried about her daughter, but she was more worried about her two grandsons. She had good reason to be worried; Sherry lived fast and loose.

Sherry and I had a great relationship; we laughed, and teased, and cut-up, but too much of what she revealed was worrisome. During one of our conversations she revealed that, until a few years ago, she considered herself a "groupie." When asked what her definition of "groupie" included, she smiled devilishly. She wasn't shy in disclosing what she did with all those musicians, sometimes more than one at a time. It's not that I was ignorant or never heard such things before—remember I owned a biker shop for over fifteen years—it's just that I liked Sherry, and I cared for her parents, and more importantly, she had two young children. I was learning Sherry's lifestyle had not changed very much; it very well could have deteriorated

Sherry's mom called one afternoon; she was extremely agitated. During our conversation, I learned the children were with her. Apparently, they had revealed much of what was going on. Her call was unexpected. My intuition, however, dictated that she was giving me warning to back away; that her daughter was beyond my help. As we spoke, her anger intensified and concluded with the assertion that her daughter was a slut. It was a difficult conversation, hearing her was difficult; the machines were noisy, and phone calls were prohibited at work, and my complete attention wasn't on the dialogue. One statement I heard plainly and caused some alarm; "I need to keep these boys," she commanded. What the boys told her, I never learned, but it had to have been explosive.

Sherry's ability to function without making some serious mistakes was triggering alarms. I was responsible for Sherry and I was becoming fearful for her safety. On one occasion, she was preparing a batter. The batter Sherry was mixing was extremely dense; consequently, the mixer needed constant attention. A constant flow of liquid was necessary to keep the batter malleable.

When I looked to check on how she was doing, she was gone. I ran to the mixer to add more liquid but it was too late. The mixing paddle broke, and that was bad, very bad. In the sixteen years that I had been a baker, I had never seen that happen. All production ceased; there was nothing we could do until we found another paddle. Sherry was apologetic, but the blame was ultimately mine.

Sherry, it seemed, was having difficulty concentrating. She had a bad cold, and it seemed to be getting worse, and so did her performance. I learned, that the sniffles and runny nose Sherry suffered was not from a cold, but rather her excessive use of cocaine, and the fatigue she suffered was due to the late-night parties. On one of our visits, Sherry's mother offered a little history; she explained that due to a hunting accident, the father of Sherry's boys was killed. She was never married to him, but lived with him long enough to be considered "common law." A considerable sum of money was awarded. Aware of how vulnerable she was to squandering her money, Sherry, asked her mother to manage it. Unfortunately, the deeper Sherry sank into drugs and immorality, the more money she demanded until there was nothing left.

The following is an account of the experience that would change the course of my life:

THE NIGHT THE
DEMONS DANCED

—————————•—————————

"SAL, CAN YOU come up here?" "What's wrong?" I answered. "Emmet accidently shot hiself." Those tragic words will forever remain locked in my memory.

That night was not unlike most other evenings. Bette cooked a great dinner, we watched some T.V., and went to bed about 9:00 p.m.

About 1:30 a.m. my daughter, Leslie, knocked on the bedroom door, "Dad...Dad...telephone; it's Sherry." Half asleep, I vaulted from my bed, my heart pounding. It had to be serious, and frankly, not unexpected.

For months, my warnings had gone unheeded, "You cannot continue to live like this; this is not a game."

Sherry was used to getting her own way. Her father sadly admitted, he bought her everything she ever wanted. Why did I think she would change on my solicitations?

"At least use some discretion for the sake of your children."

"Oh the boys love Emmet."

"Don't you understand, you can't just decide to live with a married man."

"He don't love her, besides, she's a whore." Are you any better?" I demanded.

Because of our friendship, talking with her in point blank terms was acceptable. Sometimes, however, it got a bit hot and brought strong emotion. A deep concern for Sherry was the only reason I persisted.

"Where is he shot?" I asked.

"In the head," Was her frightening reply.

There had been death threats from her old lover, Wil. Wil was a violent man.

"All through high school, it was one fight after another. Why, he'd just haul off and punch ya right in the face if he didn't like ya," a classmate, now policeman, informed me. To complicate matters, Wil had suffered severe head injuries in an auto accident, and according to neurologists, he was schizophrenic.

For Wil to learn that his ex-woman was living with his best friend. Well!

"I'm on my way." I answered into the phone.

"Be careful," was her response.

Unaware of the horrors that awaited me, I sped to get to her home. The night was so black, so still, and became more intense by my route through the unlit orange orchards. My thoughts suddenly flashed back to the conservation Sherry and I had just a week before.

"You will never believe what happened to me," she said. Not realizing the seriousness, I assured her, in a playful tone, "Sure I would." She was almost in tears, and reluctant to elaborate. That was very unusual indeed; Sherry told me everything, including some very personal intimacies. She did, however, decide to relate this strange story.

"Last night Emmet woke me. He was hysterical."

As she spoke, I noticed her eyes slowly filling. She did not appear to be sad, or angry. She was scared.

Even so, Sherry was tough. It took an awful lot to make her cry.

"He said I was talking in my sleep. Like I was having a conversation with somebody."

She stopped, walked away, then slowly walked back, but she would not allow her eyes to meet mine. She continued, "It was so weird, he wanted to leave. He was freaking out. He said it was like somebody else was talking from inside me, and then I would laugh real weird. I don't remember any of it."

When I asked if Emmet told her what she said, our eyes met very briefly, but she quickly turned away.

"Sherry, can you tell me?" I swear, I never done, I mean, well everything was about sex, I swear I never. I don't know where it came from."

She continued to elaborate, it sounded like a confession from Jack the Ripper, or Bundy. One part of this "conversation" was so heinous, she admitted, that Emmet refused to reveal it to her. I decided this "conversation" came straight from the depths of hell.

Finally, she allowed her eyes to focus on mine, they were filled with fear as well as tears.

"What's happening inside me?"

Sherry knows of my religious convictions, and she knew what I was thinking.

It couldn't be demons. I mean, well you know, it just couldn't be, I reasoned.

That conversation remained on the surface of my memory, and I met a very present reality at Sherry's home.

Everything was at an accelerated speed, until I entered that kitchen door. It seemed I was viewing everything through a movie camera. Everything slowed dilatorily, frame by frame, forward, reverse, picture by picture. Life changed for me that night.

Immediately the camera focused on Emmet. How gruesome a picture. He was clothed in jeans and cowboy boots, his bare chest expanding, contracting, struggling for each breath. The pillow on which his head rested, soaked with blood. His black hair matted with the red discharge that pumped from the hole just above his ear. The ear that would not respond to my plea. His eyes mercifully closed shutting out the emptiness within. His mouth, spuming, dripping. With each arduous breath, his body convulsed, and gave more ground.

Kneeling next to him I held his head between my hands. Pleadingly, I called, "Emmet, Emmet, if you can hear me it will be all right."

Turning his face to and from me my eyes focused on the wound. I knew then, it would not be all right. He could not survive. Not that. No one could survive that.

The odor of warm blood saturated the confines of the kitchen, so much so that it accumulated in my throat. The taste of it made me gag.

Unfortunately, the horror didn't end, it continued and grew menacingly worse.

It was vital that I call Bette. The only telephone that worked was in Sherry's bedroom. Nervously, I dialed my home, but the phone was busy. How could that be? Then it happened. I could feel my skin crawl. Chills ran up and down my body. I was trembling. There was someone in the bedroom. Behind me. I spun to meet the adversary. Not there. Where is he, or it? I questioned. Oscillating hysterically, in front of me behind me, it was all over me. I could not escape it. In my mind the words exploded, "Dear God help me!" I was terrified, but I had to get through to Bette. She had to have been frantic by now. Finally, I reached her. After putting down the receiver, I fled that room.

Whatever was in that room was ecstatic; it seemed to be in a state of elation. It, or they, seemed to be dancing.

The nefarious presence that I sensed that night afflicted me more than all the previous violations I had suffered. I had been mentally molested. Raped! I had been in the presence of a heinous evil.

Some weeks passed, and I had almost rationalized it all away when a realtor friend who had been asked to list that house called me. The story he related to me about the house, specifically, the bedroom made my hair stand. After doing his appraisal, he called. "What the blank is with that blanking house?" "Bob, is that you?" I asked. "She gave me the wrong key. I walked around that blanking house three times trying to get in. My third time around, I checked the kitchen door again, and it was open, I mean open at least six inches. If somebody was in there and ran out I would have heard them." He went on to describe the events of his walk around the interior of the house. Fortunately, he was cooling off a little. "I walked through the kitchen, and entered the living room. On the front door was the imprint of a bloody hand with dried blood that had dripped from the imprint. "But Bob," I interrupted, "the shooting happened in the kitchen. That doesn't make any sense." "Don't tell me what I saw, and what makes sense," he demanded, and continued. "Seeing that hand was bad, but what I felt in that blanking bedroom was a whole lot worse." Bob continued, "I was in combat in Vietnam at least three times. When I came home I got a job as a motorcycle cop in Lauderdale. I saw things, and been places you can't believe. I don't scare easy, but that place scared the blank out of me." I don't know what became of the house or what resided within.

Emmet died shortly after his arrival at the hospital. Because of a lack of evidence, the shooting was listed as accidental, but I don't believe it and neither do the police.

A couple of days passed when pastor Jim stopped by to visit. Our conversation included the events of that night. He listened thoughtfully, and then abruptly pronounced, "It's time to go! My first thought was that he was going to leave, but that was not his intention. He stood and declared, "I'll call the dean of students, and make the appointment. We need to get you in school." "But Jim, how am I going to pay for this?" I protested. "That's God's problem, not ours!" Was his answer, and he left.

Within the week, I found myself in the dean's office. He listened, then asked a lot of questions, again he listened. Finally, he declared, "Well, school has already begun." I was so relieved. That meant it was too late for me to enroll. I was safe. Things were happening too fast, and I was never a good student. The courses I took in high school were Industrial Arts, not Academic. I was confident I would not be attending college. The dean interrupted my reverie, and announced, "Be here Monday morning, and we'll figure this thing out. "Oh," he continued, "don't worry about the finances, we will work something out." I learned, the Southern Baptist

Convention agreed to pay one third of my tuition, and Florida Baptist College determined they would also pay one third. The remaining third would be extremely difficult; consequently, I still had my doubts.

The drive home was a blur. Pastor Jim was excited, and was talking a blue streak, but I wasn't hearing much of what he was saying. I kept thinking, "what just happened? I was a baker yesterday, and today I'm a college student." Then reality hit. OH, NO!! I'm too old to be going to college. I'm too dumb to go to college. I'll never be able to come up with the remaining one third. What about books, and travel, and gas, and housing, and the list grew exponentially.

Jim was finally able to interrupt my trance. Smiling, he informed me that the church agreed they would pay one third of my tuition. He was overjoyed to give me that news, and so was I, I think. Over and over, I kept repeating, "I'm going to college, I'm a college student, I'm going to college."

College was very difficult for me, and to think I once thought I was so smart. All thoughts of my being intellectually superior were quickly destroyed that first semester. It appeared other students found school much easier than I, yet more than half of the freshman class withdrew before their junior year. I too considered leaving, then I remembered working at the market. Oh, how I hated that job, and more importantly, how could I betray the generosity of those wonderful folks at church, and the faith of so many that was entrusted in me.

Pastor Jim's assessment of Florida Baptist College was entirely accurate. One example, as it relates directly to me: It was the policy of our Old Testament professor to give a "pop quiz," before each class. If the student was unprepared for the quiz, he/she was required to offer an explanation, in writing, before class began. My daughter had given birth to a terminally ill baby. Sadly, the baby died the evening before class. Bette nor I slept much that night; consequently, I was unprepared for the quiz. On reading my excuse, the professor asked to speak with me. During our conservation, he asked if I would be going to New Jersey, to be with my daughter. I replied in the negative. When asked why, I admitted that I was unable due to my finances. The professor excused himself from class. After a few minutes, he returned, and conducted the class. At the end of class, the professor asked that I remain for a moment. The room now empty, he approached, and handed me a check. Such was the substance and quality of Florida Baptist College and its instructors. There was yet another notable event. Bette found a lump in her breast. After an initial examination, an operation was scheduled to discover if the lump was cancer. Fortunately, it was not. Back to concentrating on school. Bette got a job working for Piggly Wiggly. She worked her way up to deli manager. I found work delivering newspapers. I also worked as a janitor for the Baptist church. My day began a two a.m. My route would end just in time for my first class, but I had to hurry. After classes, I would rush home change, and off to my second job. After about four hours, I would go home, eat supper, do my homework, and go to bed. Unfortunately, I was unable to sustain that schedule. One morning, while on my newspaper route, I became completely disoriented, I had no idea where I was. Finally, after about ten minutes of panic, everything came back. What happened, worried Bette; consequently, I resigned as janitor, and the disorientation never returned. There is much more that could be written about my college experiences, but that would be yet another book.

Well, four years after I started, I graduated Florida Baptist College with a degree in theology. I will never forget how proud Bette was. She was glowing. There was a small party; even Pastor Jim and his wife made the four-hour drive to celebrate with Bette and I. It was a glorious day. I made the comment to one fellow graduate that I had graduated high school in 1962, and I am now graduating college in 1992. His stoic reply; "If I were you, I wouldn't include that in my resume."

Resumes were sent out long before my graduation, but there were no replies. My resume was in the hands of every Director of Missions (DOM) from Key West, Florida to the northern most parts of Maine. Again, no responses. To be the pastor of a small church had become my dream. How wonderful I thought it would be. But that was not to be. Every day I would check the mail, hopeful to find an offer, but nothing. Sure, I knew I was a little abrasive, but I felt certain I could overcome that shortcoming in my personality. I knew overcoming my abrasiveness would be a major hindrance in serving as a pastor. Leaving behind my business experiences, etc., would be difficult at best, and I did have an occasional setback, but that was rare, and there was usually a good reason. At least I thought so. With some trepidation, I reveal this college experience: It was common to be teased about my Northern parlance, to which I teased back; it was all in good humor. There was, however, one student who took great joy with his banter. So much so, that it became more insult than jest. After the fourth time asking that he discontinue his slurs, I interrupted his amusement, and asked if he liked the placement of his nose. He stared and replied in the affirmative, to which I stepped forward and explained that I was about to relocate it. While he didn't know me, he did, however, sense that his nose was in some jeopardy, and backed away. Admittedly, I did feel some guilt, but I also felt more pleasure.

A friend and classmate determined if we had no responses to the many resumes each of us sent, we would continue with school and earn a graduate degree. Summer after graduation was about to end, and there were no responses. My friend, Bret, called and asked if I was ready to go back to school. Off to Troy State University, and while at Troy, I started work toward a Ph.D.

I learned the state of Florida was interviewing for the position of Forensic Chaplain. In fact, there were several chaplain's position available throughout the state. My plan was to pastor a church, but that was not in the plan of God, and I was reaching the point of desperation; I had to find employment. Resumes were sent to every Corrections facility seeking a chaplain. Fortunately, I received numerous replies. While suffering through my last Statistics class, I was called for an interview. It was a long, hot drive from our home in south Alabama to central Florida, but I was desperate for work. After what seemed an eternity, I got the call. I was going to be a chaplain. When I called Bette with the news, she promptly gave notice to her employer.

It was a long drive from our home in Alabama, to the prison in Florida. It took about six hours; fortunately, the senior chaplain knew of an apartment close to the facility which I promptly rented. The apartment permitted me to be home a couple of days a week. Those five days away from Bette, I found so difficult, but I enjoyed being a chaplain.

Working with inmates was, in many ways, like working with the customers at the motorcycle business I once owned. That same bad attitude and hateful temperament, consumed so many of them, and like the bikers, violence was always close at hand unless they needed something. When a need occurred, the bad attitude changed to one of sweetness, and hate was replaced by friendship. Oh, yes, I was home! This was the environment I was more accustomed too. Fifteen years I spent in the motorcycle business, and I got to know that narcissistic, hedonistic, personality quite well. Not to mention, at one time, I was equally guilty of similar personality defects.

A practice I incorporated early on in my ministry was to make myself available not just to the inmates, but to the officers and administration as well. It was my sense that "Institutional Chaplain," which was my title, included the institution and all who worked within. I believed if I could make it easier for an officer or the administration by tending or caring for the spiritual needs of an inmate, I would be executing the responsibilities of my ministry. It took a few months, but eventually the officers recognized I was different. They read me accurately. They knew I was not some Bible thumping pushover. They also recognized how important God's word was to me. No, I didn't act the way a "preacher" acted, I didn't talk the way a "preacher" talked, but I believed I was fair, and always willing to listen to their advice.

My chaplaincy was only in its third month when I discovered an inmate had hidden contraband in the chapel. This was a serious offense, and could have serious consequences on the operation of the chapel. The captain was immediately notified, and the inmate was sent to confinement. On visiting the inmate, he angrily demanded that chaplains didn't send chapel clerks to confinement. His rationale was that I was a man of the "cloth," as he put it, and should have given him another chance. His responsibility and guilt played no part in his punishment. "Jim" I interjected, "if you apologize for what you have done, I will happily forgive you." He immediately asked if that would get him out of confinement. My answer was no. At that, he promptly informed me what I could do with my forgiveness.

That incident may have been the turning point; the officers seemed to be more open and pleasant, and the folks in administration were always happy to see me when I made my rounds. Admittedly, I loved them, and I believe that love was reciprocal. The inmates showed me more respect, and interestingly, perhaps it was my background, or maybe they recognized I was not easily fooled by their tricks, but an inordinate number of them sought me out. They needed someone to talk to, someone who would tell them straight out what they need to hear, not what they wanted to hear. I distinctly recall their ire when during a Sunday morning message, I explained that the government of God was not a democracy, that God was the Sovereign, and there was only one way--His! I added, if they found His commands offensive, or if they determined to reject His directives, then they could all go to hell. Their reaction I even found hard to believe. A loud gasp filled the chapel. I overheard, "I can't believe the chaplain said that. Who does he think he is?" The officers, were grinning, and many of the inmates just stared at me as they exited. The following week I made it a point to mention that Jesus spoke more of hell than He did of heaven.

A practice I incorporated was to visit the confinement cells. These cells were utilized to house those inmates who were a problem. Confinement was a prison within a prison. The officer in charge would loudly announce my presence; "Chaplain in the wings," he would bellow. On one occasion, immediately after making my entrance an inmate called to me. He continued his calls, despite my demands that he had to wait his turn, and that I would not bypass him. Yet, he continued, "chaplain, chaplain, I need to talk to you, it's important." Finally, I reached his cell. The confinement cells were about 8X10 feet. Entry was through a thick steel door. A slot was fashioned in the door to permit the exchange of food or books or for conversation. This opening was made available via a door that opened from the officers' side only, and was only about 24" from the floor. There was also a very thick observation window, it measured about 12"X12." "What do you want," I asked somewhat agitated. "What does this mean," he asked, as he slid his bible through the opening. The verse in question was John 3:16; it had been highlighted in red. My first thought was he was gaming me. I came to realize he was not. His demeanor was one of urgency. Before answering, I asked that he give me some background. I learned his reason for being in confinement was well grounded. He explained he was such a bad inmate that he was not permitted residence in any institution, rather, he was transported from institution to institution allowing only a two or three day stay. This action effected by the state made it impossible for the inmate to maintain any visits with his family, or otherwise. This would also include telephone contact. He would remain in a state of isolation as long as he maintained his terrible attitude, and actions. Continuing, he explained the Bible, he thought, had been a gift from a sympathetic neighbor. He admitted to throwing it away on two occasions, but because his name was written on both covers, it followed him where ever he traveled.

He had been incarcerated for over sixteen years, and he was tired of it.

> I read the verse aloud: "For God so loved the world, that he gave his only begotten Son, that whosoever belie-veth in him should not perish, but have everlasting life," (Jn. 3:16).

I did my best to explain what those wonderful words meant. After listening to me, I remember his face contorting. He immediately stood upright, thought for a moment, then bending to the slot in the door, he asked, "What about all the people I hurt?" I explained the necessity in asking for God's forgiveness, and the requirement of sincerity. Again, he stood and contem-plated my answer. He leaned to the slot in the door asking more information. Rarely, have I seen a face so intent on hearing those words, God's words. Again, he stood upright. When he returned to that opening in the door his face was wet with tears. "Chaplain," I am confined in this tiny little room, but I have never been more free in my life." Now, tears were dropping from both of our eyes. The next day I went back, but he had already been transported to another institution. He never gave his name; I never gave mine, and I have no idea where he is or what has become of him, but it doesn't matter he is safe and secure now.

Some months later, a chaplain's position opened only an hour from home. I applied and got the job. It wasn't easy leaving that facility. It became the church I had longed for.

I learned quickly this new facility was going to be a challenge. The superintendent (warden) ran a tight ship. He was both feared and respected; I tried to stay out of his way, and managed to accomplish that for at least a month. Learning the chaplaincy took some time, much longer than the nine months I had been on the job. Fortunately, the senior chaplain, John N. was a good and kind man. He took me under his wing, and did his best to keep me out of trouble. Despite his best efforts, invariable I made mistakes.

It was a Sunday afternoon, I answered the phone, the woman on the other end was in a panic. She needed to speak with her husband. I explained the policy of the prison, to which she explained that her life was threatened by a couple of men wanting the drugs her husband had hidden. I suggested she contact the local authorities. Unsatisfied, she hung up. Thinking I was doing the right thing, I called the local authorities in her town. The individual I needed to speak with was not in, but he would return my call. A short time later I received a call from a detective assigned to this case. The conversation I had with the wife of the inmate we had in custody was given to the detective, along with the name of the inmate, the facility he was in, and the address, and telephone number of the wife. With my pride elevated, I wrote the incident report.

Anything unusual that happened in the facility had to be documented and submitted to the superintendent's office. The following morning a call came from the superintendent's office. Certain of a pat on the back, I wasted no time getting there. "Chaplain" the superintendent began, "what is your job here?" he asked red faced, eyes bulging. I was in big trouble and didn't know why. "I'm the chaplain," I answered. "What does that include?" he asked, his anger growing. "I take care of the religious needs of the institution." I answered, wiping a bead of sweat from my forehead. "Exactly!" Was his angry response. "You are not to handle any legal issues, you are not to call any police departments, you are not to speak with anyone about who is incarcerated in this institution!" After listening to more of what my responsibilities included and excluded, I was dismissed. After explaining what had happened at my meeting with the superintendent, Chaplain John was equally confused as to what I had done that was so wrong. Unfortunately, Chaplain's confusion did little to ease my discomfort. In my mind, I was unable to make sense of the superintendent's actions toward me, and I was angry about it. I felt he had no reason to treat me the way he did.

A few days after the incident, I found myself in a class designated to institutional security. The instructor was a by-the-book officer, and explained, in detail the numerous missteps I had committed. There were so many issues I was unaware of that made my actions, not only wrong but dangerous. Those dangers included, the community at large, the officers, and even other inmates.

The inmate the wife called about was the boss of a major drug cartel; he was secretly being held at our institution until the Feds could pick him up. He was noted as a serious escape risk, which included members of his organization planning and implementing such an escape. This man had extreme wealth, power and influence. I learned the call I received may have been a carefully thought out plan, for the sole purpose of learning where this man was being held so that a plan of escape could be employed. It was determined, the inmate must be relocated as quickly as possible, and, at great expense. And to think, I was angry with the superintendent. I was so ashamed.

The next day I managed to gain enough courage to visit the superintendent. The door to his office was always open. After a deep breath, I knocked and stuck my head in. He greeted me warmly, "Hey Chap. How are you today?" "I'm good, Sir. May I have a minute?" I asked. "Sure, come on in, shut the door if you like," he answered. Exactly what I said, I don't remember.

I do remember one thing I said. I asked him to for-give me. He immediately responded by saying don't give it a second thought, and he was certain I learned a lot by the experience. Included in my apology was what I believed was the more serious offense of being angry with him. The superintendent stood, grabbed my hand, and said don't worry about it, everything is good between us. He slapped me on the back and walked me to the door. I have about had it with this humility stuff!

Entering one of the dormitories, I spotted an officer. He seemed frustrated. He explained a new inmate was threatening to swallow a razorblade if his demands were not met. After spending some time with the inmate and hearing his story, I gave him my word that I would speak with the captain, and ask him to con-sider what he told me. I then asked that he spit out the razorblade. He said he would place it in my hand. Putting my hand into that cell was difficult. I prayed the inmate wouldn't slice my hand open; he didn't, he gently placed the razor on my fingertips. I immediately went to see the captain. He already knew what had happened and assured me the inmates needs would be taken care of, and they were.

It was no secret, Chaplain John was looking to retire; he was in his seventies, and had worked from the time he was a boy, he told me—on more than one occasion. When asked when? He was quick to reply, "I'm not ready just yet." It was also known the super- intendent was considering retirement. It was my third year at the prison; Chaplain called me into his office and explained, "I'm ready. You know as much as I do about this job, and before I leave, I'm going to recom- mend you to take my place as Senior Chaplain." I loved chaplain John; I was fearful to be without him.

Interviews were scheduled for the position of Chaplain. I was offered the position of Senior Chaplain. Two days later our superintendent retired. I have often wondered if he had something to do with my getting the position. There are so many stories to tell, but that would...

BAD NEWS

———————◆———————

I WAS DOING what God had appointed me to, and knowing that afforded me genuine satisfaction. And then it happened. Something was wrong. Bette's annual appointment with the doctor revealed a lump. A biopsy was needed; the biopsy revealed cancer. Breast cancer. It was the first time in our marriage I saw a trace of concern on Bette's face. Why shouldn't she be concerned; cancer afflicted both sides of Bette's family. Both her grandmothers died of the dreaded disease, one when only 38 years old. While Bette was troubled, I was terrified. Was God calling me on the vow I made so long ago?

Bette read everything she could find on alternative medicine, at the same time rejecting traditional medicine. Begging her to reconsider was futile. She had to have collected and read over five-hundred books on the subject. I was skeptical, but I relented, and learned there was some wisdom in what she proposed. I did argue, that she should consider both—alternative care and traditional medical procedures; unfortunately, my argument was dismissed, and the alternative methods were utilized.

Five years passed and Bette seemed to be thriving. With caution, I considered the possibility that the gallons of carrot juice she consumed, along with the extreme diet, the numerous supplements etc., may have worked. There were some issues that troubled me, but everything troubled me when it concerned Bette's wellbeing. She presented with several lumps on her body. One especially troubled me due to its large size. She also seemed to be having trouble swallowing. Despite these issues, she enjoyed a good appetite, she was happy, and she was very active. Gardening was something Bette enjoyed, and this spring would be no different than last. While tilling her small garden, she sprained her leg, but she managed to limp to back to the house on her own. Trying not to show how troubled I was, I teased Bette and took over for her.

Bette was in regular contact with someone who we believed was a medical doctor. According to Dr. J's book, he decided to leave traditional medicine and replace it with the significantly better, holistic medicine. Bette would call Dr. J's office in New Mexico, and make an appointment for a telephone consult, naturally there was some cost involved.

On one of his consultations, he determined the need for a blood test. Finally, a blood test, I was in full agreement; we needed to know what these lumps were. The problem I encountered was the drawn blood was to be sent to Holland. Very reluctantly, I agreed with the stipulation that I be given a copy of the blood work-up. My knowledge of medicine is very limited, but I knew enough to recognize it was worthless. On another consult, Dr. J. informed Bette of a special test he recommended. We had to drive to Louisiana. The chiropractor who conducted the test placed electrodes on Bette's hands and through a series of beeps, and bops, it was concluded that Bette was, in fact, cancer free. He did recommend another supplement.

One afternoon, while Bette was sleeping, I called Dr. J's office. I quizzed the receptionist on Dr. J's credentials. Reluctantly, she admitted he had no medical degree, Nor did he have a Ph.D. His only claim to fame: he wrote a book, which I have little doubt, was plagiarized. It is difficult to read what I have written and not conclude stupidity. Yet, Bette was very intelligent, and I would like to think I have some intellect. This begs the question: why were we so gullible? We were desperate. We believed the many testimonials of those "cured" by these uncommon procedures. Our vulnerability interfered with our common sense. I'm not suggesting Bette's life would have been spared by using traditional medicine; there is no way of knowing that, nor am I suggesting all alternative methods are worthless. I am suggesting there are some who have too few scruples.

Bette's problem with swallowing grew worse, and after much coaxing, a doctor was consulted. The diagnosis was bad, the cancer was still there, and it had spread. We also learned, the sprain Bette suffered was a fractured hip. After scrutinizing the x-ray, the doctor explained the bone that ran across the hip had a hairline crack. She touched Bette's arm and in a sympathetic tone asked how was she able to bear the pain, noting that it must be awful. Bette smiled and said it wasn't that bad and that she was managing. Bette remained very calm. Throughout her battle, I never saw her panic or cry. Completely composed, she looked at me and said, "If God wants me, I am ready. I just hope it won't be painful."

It was a long hard battle. Because I was with Bette every day, my perception of the physical changes her body was undergoing—namely loss of weight—was not as noticeable as it was to others. As long as Bette was able, we would attend church. It was the expressions on the faces of our friends that gave away how badly Bette looked from one week to the next. Even now, thirteen years later, I can see the shock fixed on their faces. So much to write; too painful to write it.

Unable to swallow, even her own saliva, I rushed Bette to the emergency room; after a brief exam, she was admitted to the hospital. This is just too damn hard! This is the reason this book has been delayed for so many years. So many tests, so many x-rays, MRI's, so many injections. The expense was tremendous. My employer provided insurance for me, but not for my spouse. It was determined Bette's cancer had grown to the point it was restricting her esophagus. A temporary fix was recommended. Bette was to have a stent positioned in her esophagus to open it. The surgeon who placed the stent was cautious to remind me it was a temporary fix. I was fearful to ask what the permanent fix would be. I remained with Bette in the hospital. Day after day, night after sleepless night, always hopeful for some news that might be encouraging. Desperately seeking hope; unfortunately, there was none to be had. It was Sunday morning, Bette was resting, and I was sitting on the chair next to her. Dr. Q knocked quietly, and entered the room. His visit was to give an update on Bette's condition. Writing this is reliving it; it is so difficult and so painful! I need a reprieve.

Once Upon a Time

———— ◆ ————

I GUESS IT'S built into our spirit or personality, a pressure valve of sorts, a way to relieve some emotional trauma. My way is to visit my memories. Oh, those memories. It is my special place, and most of the time a wonderful place. Just me and my memories. I like it there; it's temporary, I know, but while I'm there I chose what to remember. If I want, I can remember only the good stuff. Right now, I need a break, let's see where it goes.

I'm a fourteen-year-old high school sophomore, who because of failing freshman social studies must retake it. My parents had no interest in my schooling; for that matter, they didn't have much interest in anything pertaining to me.

Somewhat embarrassed, I strutted into class, looked around, and took a seat close to the door. I suppose I thought that was cool. Making the best of being a sophomore in a class filled with freshmen, I tried to act detached. As I casually scanned the class my eyes fixed on the prettiest little girl I had ever seen. Bette was a small, skinny girl, but she sure was pretty. Harry, Chuck, and Carl all thought she was too skinny. Not me, I thought she was perfect.

As the weeks went by, I made my move. There wasn't any need for a "move," Bette was so approachable, and her pleasantness extended to everyone. She would laugh at my silly jokes, and it seemed she liked me. I made every effort to be wherever she was. After school, we would meet and I would walk her home, happily carrying her books. She was so nice and she was happy. I was neither.

It was weeks before I got the courage to accept her invitation to meet her parents. My experience with parents was not very positive; consequently, I wasn't in any hurry to meet any more people who were not nice.

Bette's father was a big, strong man. He was a man's man; fishing, and hunting, and building race cars were his passions. On his way to do some repairs on his boat, he asked if Bette and I would like to tag along. I was eager to go. His boat was kept at a place called Money Island, a forty-five-minute drive. Like Bette's father, Money Island was a rugged place. It was a place where comforts were in short supply. Saw grass, marsh, a few dilapidated mobile homes, and salt water in every direction was all I saw. Finally, we were there, and he got right to work. It was a hot day, and when I looked up he was shedding his shirt. Wow! It was hard not to notice his huge muscular arms, and the six-pack he was sporting. He wasn't a talkative person, but, like his daughter, he seemed genuinely content.

Bette's mom kept a watchful eye on her daughter, especially when she came home with this Italian kid. She admitted her father didn't think highly of Italians; I suppose she inherited some of that mistrust. In my case, she couldn't be faulted. She loved and cared for her children, and it showed. That was something I wasn't accustomed to; my parents rarely knew where I was, and who I was with. While I wouldn't readily admit it, I envied the discipline in Bette's home.

Autumn gave way to winter and, in what seemed like the blink of the eye, Christmas was here. The popular songs were Brenda Lee's, *Rockin Around the Christmas Tree,* and *Chipmunk Christmas*. Our first date was on New Year's Eve. I asked if she would like to come to my house and visit. My mom and dad went out for the evening, and who knew when they would be back, certainly not before midnight. We were just kids. She was 14 and I just turned 15, December 24th. It was December 31, 1959, our first real date. I was so excited. There could be no doubt, even at that age, I knew I genuinely loved Bette. She had a purity, and an innocence, that I envied and wanted. I was more aware, when I was with Bette, I felt safe, playful, inno-cent. Why I felt that way, I'm not certain. Perhaps, it was how sure she was of herself, or her independence, maybe it was her purity. It seemed she knew how to act, and knew what to do in any given situation. It was instilled within her, it just came naturally. In contrast, I followed the lead of others; if sadness was the appro-priate expression, I became sad, if happiness, then I would laugh, etc. Yet, I believed, the performance I gave presented me as authentic. The time went by so fast, Bette had strict orders to be home by 10:00 p.m. It was a cold night; we shivered, and we giggled as we walked to her home. I kissed Bette goodnight (our first kiss), and went straight home, a happy boy. Later that night 1960 came. Who could have known Bette would become my wife in four short years?

Bette became my instructor, and yet, she was unaware of the education she was furnishing. My learning included being nice was okay, but it took me years to be nice. School nights, I was permitted to be with Bette Monday and Wednesday, but I had to be on my way by 8 p.m. Saturday's, we tried to be together as early we could, but curfew was 11:00 p.m. If it snowed, we played in it; if it rained, we walked in it. When it was hot and humid we walked to the lake. I was alive when I was with her. I could be a kid, and it was fun being a kid. The trouble was, I had to go home. That wasn't fun.

Bette babysat for what money she had. One of her regulars was her aunt. Apparently, there had been an hourly fee for Bette's services, but too often she didn't get paid. To Bette, it didn't matter. When I learned, she worked for nothing, I became angry and thought she was being taken advantage of. Bette thought nothing of it. Through the year, she would put the little money she made aside. With some of the money, she bought girl stuff, but with most of her money, she bought gifts. It was Christmas and Bette asked if we could go shopping together. I never bought anything for anybody before. Giving, was another thing Bette taught me.

She had a list, aunts, uncles, parents, etc. So many people to buy gifts for, I thought she must have made a lot more money babysitting than I realized; she didn't. A dollar here, two dollars there, etc., etc. In short order, each name had a check next to it. I was amazed, still am. Pitman, N. J., that's where we did "our" shopping, there were no malls built yet; in fact, no one knew what a Mall was. It was so cold that day in November. I can still hear the Christmas carols resonating up and down Broad Street. I remember every shop we went into; I remember how much fun we had. Yeah, I remember, I remember it like it was yesterday.

BACK TO THE PRESENT

———◦———

"GOOD MORNING," DR. Q. began, "I'm so sorry to tell you this, but the cancer has spread. I'm afraid it's everywhere: her spleen, her breasts, her liver, her…" I fell back into the chair. Doctor Q stopped, and once again expressed his sympathies. Shattered, I asked, "How long do you think she has doctor?" Words have always held a fascination for me, but the word Dr. Q used was such a common word. Certainly, no significance could be associated to it. I could relate to words like: engaged, or married, husband, or father. Now those are words with depth, they have significance. They have value and worth, but "Days?" Until that Sunday morning in June, the word "days" held little significance, but that morning, that morning it became a word of monumental significance. "DAYS." How many "days?" Two, five, eight, how many "days" will I have my

Bette? Surely, he's wrong. He's mistaken. God wouldn't do that, would He? Why wouldn't He? Bette was on loan to me, she taught me what she could, and now her contract completed, her Father wanted her back. The hand that held tight the seat of my bicycle was now released; I am on my own.

"Was that the doctors voice I heard?" Bette asked, in her weakened state. "Yes," I answered, knowing what the next question would be. "Well, what did he say?" she asked. There was no other question that could be asked, that was it and there was nothing to answer but the truth. "It's bad." I answered, again aware of what the next question would be. "How bad?" she asked. "Bette," I answered, "it's as bad as it could be." "How long do I have?" If we were brave enough, or honest enough, I suppose that question would be the one everyone would ask, but no one has the answer. Except today, I have it, the answer. "The doctor," I began, "said," here's that damn word again, "days." As if nothing had transpired, Bette asked, "What are you going to do with me?" "What do you mean," I asked? It was unnerving, what could she mean? "Will you have me buried or cremated?" Two factors made this conversation inconceivable, the first simpler than the second. The question, just as it stands, seems so inappropriate. Now, you ask such a question? Here, in this place you ask me a question of such enormity; "Bury or cremate?" And the questioner is the one to whom the answer applies. Couldn't this wait? No, it couldn't. "Days," remember?

There is a second element in Bette's inquiry. It is the most revealing, and holds the greatest consequence. Hidden within Bette's question is one, seemingly insignificant word. That word represents the greatest change in our relationship. Listen again to the question; "what are YOU going to do with me?" "We" exited the room; the only one remaining was "me." For forty years, it was "we." In that hospital room that morning it suddenly changed from "we" to "me." From here on, there was no more "we." All responsibility would be mine, and It didn't matter if I was ready. It was all on me!

The need to change the subject was overwhelming. "I'm thirsty," I said. "Would you like some water?"

Bette's eyes followed me. As I grabbed the pitcher, my knee gave; I almost fell. Steadying myself, I looked at Bette, my face wet with tears. "I can't bear to lose you," I demanded! Her expression was one of compassion, and love, yet firmly she answered, "You had better toughen up!" I poured us some water, walked back to her bedside and sat down. Bette had expressed her desire to be cremated many months ago. In my answer to her question, I explained if she were buried, I would need to stay in Mississippi, however, if she would be cremated, I could move to North Carolina. Both my son, Ken, and daughter, Natalie, lived in the same town, and Bette would come along. "Then it's settled," she explained, "I'll be cremated." She was satisfied, smiled and took a sip of her water. In a state of bewilderment, I, too, sipped my water.

A few minutes passed when Rodger C., our pastor knocked and entered Bette's room. Bette felt no appre-hension in revealing Dr. Q's finding, and prediction. Rodger explained he was leaving for vacation later that afternoon. He was headed to visit his relatives in one of the New England states--which one I can't recall. He added, "please call me if anything happens, and I'll come right back." Bette smiled, and explained she wasn't going anywhere just yet. Our conversation was quite common. There was no drama, no show of crisis. There would be more drama if we were discussing politics.

A few days passed and Bette was released from the hospital, her condition grave. Honored and privileged, I cared for Bette's every need; consequently, I left the house only when necessary. Swallowing was still the major issue. Sadly, Bette's menu had been narrowed to applesauce and a few sips of carrot juice. One afternoon, laboring over her applesauce, she decided to talk about her condition. Trying to avoid anything too serious, I playfully, offered, "You have to get well because I'm too old to find another woman." With unmeasured compassion, Bette looked in my eyes, tried to smile and said, "If you do, I'm sure she will be wonderful." With that, she asked that I help her get back in bed. As I reasoned what had just transpired, I grasped the character of this wonderful lady. Had circumstances been reversed, it's not likely I would have been so charitable.

It was hard for me to get past Bette's words. It was Bette I wanted, and needed. We had six wonderful children together. While I was so negative, she was so positive. When worry overcame me, Bette was a cradle of encouragement. It was she who worked and helped me through college, graduate school, and post graduate school. It was Bette who made a man of me, and on and on, and on. I needed a reprieve, to lose myself for a while. Evoking the past serves as an ideal escape. Physically, I may be nearby, but emotionally I'm lost in my memories.

Because of my mother's mental illness, much of her life was spent in institutions designated to treat emotional disorders. My first recollection of a mental breakdown: I was five or six years old. The car pulled up to a massive building. It must have taken up a whole city block; its name, Byberry State Hospital. It is so strange that I would remember the name of that place so many years ago. I couldn't understand why I was in uncle's Bill's car, and not riding with my mother and father. Aunt Rose chimed in; "Don't worry honey, it's going to be okay." That was the first alarm. Two men approached my father's car. Their all white uniforms frightened me, and then they did the unthinkable. They forced my mother out of the car. She was screaming and pleading for help. They put a coat on her; it tied from the back. I learned the coat was a straight-jacket. Uncle Bill, and my father just watched; Aunt Rose did her best to shield my eyes and comfort me. I didn't understand. I was hysterical and begged for my mother.

Over the years, I developed an immunity to my mother's continual trips to mental hospitals. Some were state institutions and some privately owned. Every known treatment was dispensed, from shock treatments to hundreds of hours of counselling. Every form of treatment was ordered, including hundreds of psychotropic drugs, none of which rendered a remedy. Throughout my life, my mother was either sick or getting sick. My contempt for her grew with each passing year. For my father, I felt some pity, but more anger, that he would not or could not stop her insanity. It would be reasonable to determine my life was devoid of parental care or concern, and that was just fine with me. I learned to take care of myself. When I needed clothes, I stole them. If my clothes needed washing, I washed them in the bathtub, often, wearing them while still dripping wet. That was fine in the summer months, but winter? Working in the bakery was my one requirement. When my work was completed, I wasn't seen until the next morning. I became an angry person, and then there was Bette.

Bette and I did a lot of double-dating, sometimes we would take the bus to the movies. The Broadway Theater in Pitman, N.J. had the best shows. When I turned seventeen, it was my driver's license that was the first order of business. Not long afterward, I bought my first car: a 1959 Chevy, convertible. It was white with red interior; I loved it, but I was in love with Bette. Every Monday, we would head to the shore; that was my day off. We would get an early start, and we would be off. Avalon, N.J. was our destination. It was such a fun time. Bette loved laying in the sun. After a couple of hours, I was ready to go; I wanted to drive. Driving was something I truly enjoyed; from Wildwood, N.J. to Cape May Court House, the wind in our hair—I did have black hair back then, lots of it. I miss hair!

In school, I made sure to pass all my classes; Bette wanted me too. At seventeen, I graduated; it was 1962. My eighteenth year, I especially remember. It was not a good year for me. I started to have dreams. These dreams seemed to be of future events, and I didn't like what I was seeing. Too often, I would wake up breathless, and trembling, sweating profusely. Reluctantly, I told Bette about the dreams, and their effect. Worried, she made an appointment with a doctor she found in the yellow pages. Because of Bette's urging, I agreed to go, wondering what I was going to tell him. Doctor Lovelace was a great guy, and he cared. The first thing he did was take my blood pressure. He went no further. "Do you have insurance," he asked. "No," I answered, "but I can get it." His reply came quickly, "It's too late now my friend, your blood pressure is extremely high; you need to be in the hospital." After explaining to him the impossibility of a hospital stay, he made me promise to visit a doctor friend of his. Well, a promise is a promise. Bridgton, N.J. is where Dr. Irving S., the internist, had his office. After a battery of tests, Dr. S. asked a question I thought was very strange, "What the hell is your problem, young man?" "I thought you were supposed to tell me," I answered. With a serious look on his face he affirmed, "Every test you have been given indicates you are in excellent physical condition. So, again I ask, what the hell is wrong with you?" After, what seemed like hours of consultation, Dr. S. explained, "You're a pretty smart kid; unfortunately, people like you either accept the world as it is, or you will have a very miserable existence." It's been years, and I still struggle with accepting things I cannot change, besides how do you accept a belief that the country you love will collapse.

Bette graduated high school in 1993. Hairdressing was something she enjoyed, and after searching the yellow pages found the right school. She graduated from the Jar-Dan school of Hairdressing and Cosmetology in Camden, N. J. It went out of business years ago. She was soon employed by Lit Brothers department store, also in Camden, N.J. (Lit Brothers closed its doors in 1977). Bette saved her money and bought a Volkswagen bug. She enjoyed being a beautician. Bette found enjoyment in almost everything she did; it didn't take much to make her happy.

PREGNANT?
PREGNANT! PREGNANT.

————————◆————————

WHEN BETTE TOLD me, I was terrified. Pregnant? Maybe she was wrong? Dr. Lovelace confirmed Bette's condition, "Yep, your pregnant." (Bette and I both loved Dr. Lovelace. He affectionately named Bette, Princess. A few years after delivering our second child he died of cancer; he was very young). Now what? Bette informed her mother, and she was understandably hurt. We became husband and wife December 5th, 1964.

It's time for me to check on Bette. Some months back she made me promise I wouldn't hover over her while she slept. She explained it would make her uncomfortable knowing I was watching her. She caught me once; I apologized. She smiled and said, "I know I told you not to hover, but it's okay, I love it." With each passing day, Bette spent more time in bed. She wanted to sleep more and more. She was always a small woman; I doubt she weighs eighty pounds now. The doctor's prescriptions included something for pain and something to make her sleep; more often she would ask for the pill to help her sleep. Going to church was now out of the question. "Would you like me to stay and keep you company?" I asked. "No, I'm fine, that pill works pretty fast. I'm okay. You go ahead," she answered. Conflicted. Wanting to stay just to be near her, but not wanting to make her feel uncomfortable, I honored her request. Feeling helpless, and very aware of how critical Bette's condition was, my refuge became my memories; I longed to revisit our past.

Sure, I was scared, three weeks before we were to be married my father informed me he could no longer afford to keep me on. So, I was getting married to my pregnant Bette, and now I was unemployed. Every day I would scan the newspapers looking for work; I was hopeful.

We drove my Buick convertible—I had traded my Chevy a couple of months earlier—and headed to the Pocono Mountains for our honeymoon. Our destination, Mount Airy Lodge. It was only a weekend, but it was a terrific couple of days. I vividly remember the desk clerk asking me to write our names in the registry. That was the first time I saw our names written as Mr. and Mrs. It was wonderful. I couldn't help but take a second look.

A young man escorted us to "our" room. After he put "our" bags on the bed he held out his hand. I quickly gripped his hand and gave it a very brisk shake. How could I know he was waiting for a tip? We were just a couple of kids, she eighteen and I nineteen. We bounced on the bed, checked out every drawer, and soon realized we were hungry. Bette's father gave us $100, so the sky was the limit. We found the dining room okay, but there were only two entrees on the dinner menu, filet mignon and filet of soul. We looked at each other, shrugged our shoulders, and picked the one that didn't sound like a shoe; the filet mignon was wonderful.

It was the close of a very busy day, and we were exhausted. It seemed sleep came for Bette instantly, but not for me. There was someone in my bed, and she smelled like hairspray. Fearful of waking Bette, I determined not to move; I lay there like a statue. Morning came. We hoped the breakfast menu would be more understandable. It was, we both knew what bacon and eggs were. Bette nor I knew how to ski—good thing, we had no money. We walked and we played in the snow. Lunch was passed over—we needed to save the little money we had for the filet mignon. We were on the road early Sunday morning. I was scheduled for an interview with Owens Corning Fiberglass in Barrington, N.J. Factory work was different from anything I have ever done. Paired up with a fellow from Georgia, the foreman gave the two of us, what seemed a job that made no sense to either of us. We were instructed to move a large pile of sand from under a huge oven to another place under that same oven about forty feet away. Anxious to prove our worth, we finished the job in short order. The foreman was surprised at how quickly we got the job done. "Well," he said, "let's see what else we can find." After an hour, he approached. "Come with me," he said. Leading us back under that oven he explained, "Boys, I need you to put that sand back where you got it." Do you understand?" We thought we understood, but we had no idea. Once again, thinking if we worked hard and fast, we would prove our worth. Proudly, we informed the boss we had completed the task. The foreman took a deep breath, shook his head and explained there was a plant lay-off, and because I was a new employee, I was one of the first to go. By the time the lay-off was over, I had found another job.

Blackwood Bakery, I was baking again. Working my way to first hand baker had its advantages, and a few disadvantages. Another baker thought he should have been offered the position. After all, he reasoned, I was much too young to hold that position. He was at least five years older; therefore, the job should be his. The boss rejected his reasoning; consequently, my position remained secure Baker, First Class. Unfortunately, "angry second-hand baker" refused to do a good job, and the responsibility of his blunders fell on me. Explaining to "angry second-hand baker" the consequences of his deliberate blunders changed nothing. Unfortunately, it became necessary to explain my situation to him in a more forceful manner. The parking lot was a good place to give "My Explanation." After he cleaned himself up in the bathroom, "angry second-hand baker" called, the boss. Charley was not happy to be disturbed at two-thirty a.m. After giving my side, Charlie demanded, "I do not condone fighting in my bakery." Then he smiled broadly and said, "Damn, I wish I was here." He did make me clean up the blood in the bathroom. I was certain I was going to be looking for another job, but, thankfully, I didn't.

CHRISTMAS

———————•———————

A FEW WEEKS after our marriage it was Christmas. Wanting to surprise Bette, I bought our first Christmas tree without her—she was at work. That proved to be a mistake. It was a big tree, a really big tree! It was our first Christmas, and I wanted it to be special. The tree was at least 15 feet tall, and about 8 feet at its widest place. The trunk was about 8 inches. What was I thinking? By the time I finished cutting and trimming, more than half of it remained in the back yard. Bette laughed so hard, she couldn't catch her breath. After getting over my embarrassment, I laughed too. We were so happy, so very happy.

Bette called the bakery; her water broke. I wasn't exactly sure what that meant. Bette explained it was time for the baby to come. Neither the ride home or the ride to the hospital do I remember. What I do remember is Bette hurting, and I didn't like it. Finally, the nurse came into the waiting room, and called my name. Smiling she explained I was the father of a healthy baby boy, and would I like to see him. "No!" I said, "I want to see my wife. The expression on her face gave away her disbelief to my answer. Everyone in the waiting room was startled with my answer. The nurse assured me Bette was fine. I thanked her, but my answer remained the same; "I want to see my wife first." At that moment, Bette was the only thing that mattered. Fifteen minutes later, I was escorted to Bette side. I don't recall Bette ever looking so beautiful as she did at that moment. Satisfied she was fine, I asked to see my son. Now there were two words linked to me, "Husband, and father;" I was both. In addition, I have a "son." Guess that makes it three words? Bette was so healthy, so happy, and so beautiful.

Avoiding the board that squeaks loudly, I made my way into the bedroom. Bette is resting quietly. While healthy and happy no longer apply, her beauty endures. As the end nears, writing becomes more difficult. With every word I write I know I am approaching death, Bette's. To avert or delay writing of Bette's death can only work for so long. Bette is sleeping. She seems comfortable.

One evening, after prayers, Bette took my hand and thanked me for being a good husband. She continued and said something I had wanted to hear all our married life; "I need you," she admitted. So many times, I expressed my need for her, she would always answer with, "I love you." Never with, I need you too, but that night...

As I write, I realize I am not able, no, not just yet. Bette's last moments, even now, thirteen years later are so vivid, so painful. The difficulty is much more than I realized, and the good memories are so enticing. Now, where was I? Using my Buick as a down payment, we managed to buy a house. We were so proud. The house was old, but nice. It had two pillars separating the living room from the dining room. It furnished a look of grandeur. It was a two-story home. The upstairs had been converted to an apartment. The rent from the apartment conveniently paid our mortgage.

Our second winter: It was late November, and it was cold. The bakery was humming; folks were placing orders for their favorite Thanksgiving treats. Pumpkin, and mince pie orders were always high on the list. The holidays meant more work for me, but I was used to it; I had been a baker most of my early life, and despite my family situation, the joy of the season was contagious.

Tired, hungry, and cold I pushed my way through the back door. Bette greeted me with a kiss and a smile. From where I was standing, I could see a small portion of the living room, and it was beautiful. The reflection of those wonderful little lights circling the pillars separating the living room from the dining room was simply amazing. Bette had decorated our home for Christmas. It was perfect; it was Christmas in my house. It reminded me of the department store windows in Philadelphia. Bette had been saving for some months, and bought all sorts of Christmas decorations. Yes, It was Christmas, it was my house, and my wonderful wife did it. I was the luckiest guy in the world. What a house. What a wife.

My mother's mental collapses were, too often, cal-
ibrated with some holiday; unfortunately, Christmas
had the distinction of being the holiday of highest significance; consequently, Christmas became a holiday I
did not look forward to, it was a day of rage and resentment, followed by the inevitable trip to the mental
institution. I desperately wanted Christmas to be the
joyful holiday it was supposed to be, instead Christmas,
and the days leading up to it, became a horror for me.
So many evenings, I would be poised at the top step,
primed to reach the kitchen quickly, certain my father
would kill my mother in a fit of rage. For days, she
would deprive him of sleep with her unrelenting con-
flict. No one, I reasoned, could hold up under that tor-
turous treatment. One night they were engaged in a
terrible battle. I was fourteen years old, at the time. I
heard the drawer open, and I heard silverware moving.
Certain, he was going to take a knife from the drawer,
to use on her, I leapt down the stairs as quickly as I
could. Confronting my father, I grasping his arm, and
shouting for him to stop, he threw me across the room
like a rag doll. It was then I noticed he was holding a

spoon, not a knife. He ran at me, put his fist to my face and screamed for me to get out.

What a wonderful contrast. My home looked like a Christmas wonderland, and my wonderful wife made it happen. Included in those decorations, was the understanding of what the celebration of Christmas was all about. My education was progressing. Numerous times I questioned why God was so gracious to me. I was certainly not worthy of Bette. Years later, I sharing that question with my daughter, Natalie, she answered without the slightest hesitation, "Dad it's because God knew you needed mom more than anyone else." God had, and has blessed me with many gifts, the greatest is certainly His forgiveness. That forgiveness, I learned, was available through Bette's teaching me about the true Savior.

THE GREAT CONTRAST

———————◆———————

IT WAS BECOMING more obvious; Bette wasn't going to get well it certainly wasn't for a lack of prayer, or a lack of faith. There were many who offered their heart-felt prayers on Bette's behalf. Some learned of Bette's cancer from the monthly newsletter I send out, and certainly, the members of the church Bette and I attended offered their prayers. As to Bette's faith, she never wavered, (Romans 8:28). Unfortunately, Bette was no longer resting comfortably; her breathing was labored due to the congestion in her chest. As I sat watching her every movement, I began to contrast my mother with my Bette.

The very word <u>mother </u>moves most people to feelings of warmth, love, affection, and security. For the most part, tender memories are aroused. How badly I wish I too could share in those forms of remembrances;

unfortunately, I cannot. Memories of my mother are painful.

I see her in many ways, but never as mother. I visualize her screaming with the fury of hell; her eyes glaring, and enraged. Her exchanges were, too often, mean, and vicious, rarely happy. She was always critical, never positive. When she wasn't in a mental facility, she was a tyrant, barking out orders, and shouting obscenities. Sadly, these fits of rage were common. Night was more severe; it was my enemy. Screams and constant arguing were the norm. Unable to sleep, She would continue for days, keeping my father up around the clock, and too often, me as well. It was then we knew, it was time to take her away.

I can still, even now, see her sitting alone in that empty, antiseptic room staring into the emptiness. So sad a picture, so lonely, so alone, and so unable to function. On many occasions, I watched my father feed her like a baby. He would place the food into her mouth, and sadly, it would fall into her lap.

Once while visiting her, I asked, "Mom, please tell me what you are thinking," her mouth would open and close, her lips moving, but there was no sound. The exercise continued until her frustration forced her to stop, her eyes pleading for some relief.

Admittedly, seeing her like this tore at my heart; I suppose, it still does. So, helpless, and in such terrible mental anguish. Behold, my mother with her pleading eyes! I often think of that old analogy of the glass of water being half full or half empty. The concept: the optimist will see the glass half full, while the pessimist will see it half empty. My opinion—that analogy holds no verity. Combining my education with my experience, I have seen on many an occasion an individual having his/her glass overflowing, yet they will be angry and lack contentment. Too often this lack of contentment has nothing to do with an offense committed against them. Unfortunately, it is because they want it that way. Ridiculous? I believe not.

The problem, as I see it, resides within all mankind. The bible tells us all man has sin; it's in our DNA for heaven's sake. I believe, included in that DNA is a place. I'll call it a drawer in our brain. There are hundreds, maybe millions of drawers there, but this particular drawer is one we go to in times of great stress. This drawer was discovered long ago, while we were very young. Let's assume, an event took place that caused much worry or trauma. Age made it impossible to avoid that stress, and may have caused the event to be worse than it was. Trapped in that awful circumstance, the search begins; the search to find a release. Every drawer is opened, and searched. An escape must be established. Finally, a relief is located; it serves as a substitute; it temporarily replaces the stress. Some will seek and find in that drawer a method of relief that will be beneficial, both to the individual, and, possibly the situation. Another will find a less productive substitute: it may be manipulation, or screaming, or banging their head on the floor, or holding their breath, any number of practices are employed until they find the one that works best. Counseling with one inmate, he admitted at the age of five he found his "drawer," unfortunately, it was the drawer of immorality. He located that drawer shortly after his parents divorced. Since its discovery, his use of it became his obsession, his fantasy. He succumbed to his fetish, and is imprisoned for multiple rapes.

Admittedly, the variables are endless; consequently, locating the "drawer," allows for a limited or, continuous use. The glass of water, half full or half empty is of no consequence. For some the drawer remains forever open. Its use becomes habitual, sadly habit turns to dependency, dependency transforms to fixation, and fixation to obsession.

In Bette's case, when some stressor overwhelmed her, the drawer she found kindness, and peace, calmness and love. In contrast, my mother's choice was strife and anger, provocation, and manipulation. My mother should, and could have been happy at almost any place in her life; Unfortunately, she chose to be miserable. To exacerbate this condition, she demanded everyone near her to be of the same temperament.

To offer just one example: due to an illness, my father had to spend some time in the hospital. In his absence, I took over the bakery—without my assuming the responsibility the bakery would have closed. My mother made every effort to make my life like hers— miserable. Hour after dismal hour, she sparred with me throwing her cutting jabs. She knew every move.

Surely, I reasoned, she will tire of her abuse, but she didn't. She was a professional, I was a novice. Thinking I would be forced to assume the extra work, she fired, without reason, one of our best sales girls. Mary had been with the bakery for over fifteen years. I informed my mother I would not take on the extra work, and that she would bare the added responsibilities; Mary was promptly rehired.

It seemed she was failing in her attempts to bring me down, and I was proud of myself. Silly me, she was just preparing for the big punch. In my mind, I reasoned, I would not allow her to do to me what she did to my father, but she was equally determined. Unwavering, she probed for any weakness; she accused me of awful things. When that had no effect, she accused my children of terrible offenses. Keep in mind, she was their grandmother yet, she was berating them. Add to that, if I were to walk out, the financial losses would be catastrophic.

I was beginning to weaken, but I was determined not to allow her victory. Unfortunately, she was equally determined, and she was the champ. The unceasing assault was taking a toll. Trolling, probing, anxiously seeking to appease that damn "drawer." Finally she found it; she probably knew it all along; "and that g__ damn whore you call a wife," that was as far as she got. I ran at her screaming, and in that moment, I realized, she got me, and I remembered my father's words, "you have no idea what or who she is." Screaming at her, I shouted, "you are an evil woman, and one day you will be all alone."

She died in a nursing home, alone, and no, I didn't attend her funeral. It's sad knowing happiness was right there for the taking, but she was addicted to that "drawer." No, I didn't hate her, but I sure as hell didn't like her. Compassion, pity, sympathy, these are the words that best describe the feelings I have for her, the lady with the pleading eyes. As for love, sadly, I think not.

The Angels come

———————◆———————

IT WAS ABOUT 2:30a.m. Bette woke me asking for my help. It was common for Bette to wake up in need of help at least once during the night. As I sat on her bedside, she bolted upright with amazing speed, before I could respond, she shouted, "I can't breathe!" Putting my arm around her, she slumped foreword; she was gone. I begged. I pleaded. I prayed. I cried. My Bette was gone. She was no longer my Bette, now, as she had always been, she was God's Bette.

The paramedics came, the police came, the coroner came, the neighbors were awakened by the noise and the lights, never has my home been so filled with so many people so early in the morning, and yet, I was alone; "we" became "me" for the final time that night, and it was permanent, and it was irreversible. People were talking, and telling stories, some were laughing out loud. They were just being people. I was alone. For a moment, I thought I wanted to die; to be with Bette, but, I knew I couldn't. Giving in to my grief was not an option; I had phone calls to make, and I must be strong. Each of my children were notified, and each one managed their sorrow and pain differently. Collectively, the greatest fear they shared was for me. They knew where the strength of their parent's union rested, and she was gone. It was now only me, and my children feared for their father.

Some of the events of that morning I remember vividly others, a blur. The paramedics arrived within minutes after my call. They asked if I wanted them to try to revive Bette; no, was my response. I remember they covered Bette's face with a blanket. I had to leave the room. A few minutes passed, and I had to go back to my Bette. The paramedic was still with Bette. I asked if could take the blanket from Bette's face, "of course," was her answer. I did; Bette no longer looked like Bette; consequently, I was forced to replace the blanket and I left our/my bedroom. From where I was sitting, in the den, I heard an unusual noise, one I had never heard before, but one I will never forget. It was the rattling of the gurney going down the hallway with Bette on it. She was leaving me forever. I knew I would never see her again. A pain I am unable to express consumed me, and I sobbed for a long time. Everyone left: the paramedics, the police, the coroner, the funeral director, even the neighbors. More importantly, Bette had gone.

Except for Ken, who was physically unable, all my children, their children, and their spouses, came. There was food everywhere, and there were people everywhere. Seeing them interact with each other, coming into the living room to check on me was all so wonderful. During all the food and soft drinks, and clamor, I heard a knock. At first I thought it was one of the kids; it was not. Again, the knock. Leslie, my daughter, also heard it. I started toward the door when, a sorrow so extreme and so intense, stopped me, and I fell against the wall. I watched as the funeral director gave to Leslie a box. The box, its contents; my wife.

Reluctantly, Leslie extended her hand and I accepted the "cremains." Leslie's face revealed her grief. "Cremains," I absolutely hate that word almost as much as the word "cancer." Yesterday, I was attending to my wife as she lay in her bed. Today, she is represented by a 6 x 6 square box. Yesterday, at this exact time, I was stroking her hair, offering her water, talking to her, today I am holding a cardboard box. How did I bear it? I am unable to bare it now. As I lay in bed that night, (on Bette's side) I felt a measure of comfort: first, I knew Bette was not in that box, second, I knew where Bette was, and third, I allowed myself to believe that two angles had perched themselves on the wall above the closet. At the appointed time, they approached one took Bette by the hand the other led the way upward. As they presented their prize, the Father declared, "Well done thou good and faithful servant." It's true, that's what I want to believe, but I think I'm close.

Enduring those first few days, was made possible because my children were there with me. The thought of their leaving me to go on with their lives was a painful thought, but one I had to accept. Leslie and Holly left for their homes in Florida, and Connie left for Georgia. Natalie, my youngest daughter, stayed as long as she could, but she too had to leave. Michael, my youngest, lived with Bette and I, but he too would be leaving me.

ALONE!

———◆———

WAVING, AS NATALIE pulled away, panic struck. I was alone, completely alone. What was I going to do? Should I stay in our home, there is no "<u>our</u>" any more, it's just my home. Should I sell my home? Should I rent a place to live in? Should I move away from Mississippi? What should I do? Where should I go? My head was spinning. I need to talk to Bette but Bette is no more; it's just me. I missed my children. I was so confused, and so alone. Everything my eyes focused on, I saw Bette. Everything I touched, brought a memory of my Bette, and the realization that Bette is no longer mine.

Rarely did I leave the recliner she sat in. It was next to the fire place. The fire place she so enjoyed watching. It was too much, too many things, my head was hurting. I realized I was in trouble. There was a loud shout, more like a scream; it was me! I was coming apart, and I had to stop it! In my mind, I determined, I will survive this. I will be fine! First, and foremost, I am not alone. I was promised "I will never leave or forsake you." No, He would never leave me, and I had my children. I could talk to them anytime I needed. There were my friends, and there was my job.

TIME LESSENS THE HURT

———————◆———————

TODAY IS JULY 1. Thirteen years today Bette died. "Died," another word added to my repartee, funny how I avoid using that word. "Passed away," had been the preferred terminology. Is it because "passed away" doesn't sound so permanent? Perhaps it's more "Christian?" I don't know, silly me.

Yes, I've remarried , and yes, I married a "wonderful" woman; just like Bette had predicted. Sure, time has lessened the pain, but in reality, it's only a memory or two away and, after all, a part of Bette resides within each of my children. In any case, my story has taken an unexpected urgency. June 12th, 2004, Bette was admitted to the hospital, July first, Bette died. Thirteen years later, June 14th I was admitted to the hospital. The doctors statement, "Sal, you have had a major, major heart attack." Three stents had to be placed in my artery to open it. On August 17th, I underwent surgery to have a defibrillator/pacemaker installed. Today is August 19th. Bette would have celebrated her seventy-second birthday today.

I am currently in the Broad Street Café, writing and waiting for Karen. She is in the hairdresser, having her hair done. And, no, I'm not feeling very well. My chest is throbbing from the incision, and my heart doesn't feel just right. All things being what they are, I suppose it's time to end my story. Sure, I have been told that many folks who have had similar conditions live long and productive lives. Perhaps, I too will enjoy a similar outcome. If that would seem to be the case, I may just write another book.

A note from Karen:

———————◆———————

STEVE, DECIDED TO do some landscaping—we were planning to build. I reasoned that he must have gotten tired and was enjoying his solitude as he always enjoyed camping. Now it was morning and he was still not home. I decided to go to the site. His truck was there, but he was not answering my calls.

All my years as an RN, and all my training did not nor could not prepare me for what I saw. My husband lying there in the middle of that smoldering brush, burned to death, almost beyond recognition. I know I was screaming, but I didn't hear a thing. That was March, 2004. Just ten months later my daddy, whom I dearly loved died. I hadn't had sufficient time to grieve the death of my husband. We had been married twenty-eight years and had two wonderful children together; now my Father. Four years earlier my younger sister died of brain cancer; she was only forty years old. I was hurting!

My friend, Barb was visiting me regularly; she suggested I talk with her boss. She reasoned, he was a trained counsellor, and had recently lost his wife to cancer. I was already speaking to a counsellor. I agreed, but demanded I was not interested in dating, or for that matter any relationship.

Sal called. For the next few months we talked on the phone. Once a week or so we would talk. It was just small talk: how are you doing today, are you eating, going to church, etc. We finally agreed to meet. Well, we met in the Target parking lot. I got in my Mustang but it wouldn't start. Oh, no! The only thing that ran was Steve's pickup. Here I come driving up in this big 4X4 with these huge mud tires. Oh well, it's just coffee.

On more than one occasion I explained that I was not interested in any kind of a relationship, Sal just smiled. I'll never forget that one special night, "Karen" he began, "I'm going to marry you." "Don't say that again or I'll leave, you're pretty sure of yourself" I demanded. His answer, "I know my heart, and I know my God, and this is no mistake, you will marry me one day."

While attending church one Sunday morning I distinctly felt in my spirit, my God speaking to me. Sal was sitting next to me and my Lord and Savior was telling me to quit fighting His will. Sal was to be my husband. I knew it was He who gave me this man.

we just celebrated twelve wonderful years of marriage and it never ceases to astound me how Our Lord gives us peace that surpasses all understanding when we obey Him. I am honored to share this life with my Salvatore and I am grateful for my Father God's love.

CPSIA information can be obtained
at www.ICGtesting.com
Printed in the USA
LVOW12s2148110518
576896LV00001B/142/P